NEW YORK JETS · SUPER BOWL CHAMPIONS

III, JANUARY 12, 1969

16-7 VERSUS BALTIMORE COLTS

SUPER BOWL CHAMPIONS

NEW YORK JETS

AARON FRISCH

CREATIVE EDUCATION

COVER: QUARTERBACK JOE NAMATH

PAGE 2: THE JETS DEFENSE PLAYING IN SUPER BOWL III

RIGHT: QUARTERBACK VINNY TESTAVERDE AND COACH BILL PARCELLS

Published by Creative Education
P.O. Box 227, Mankato, Minnesota 56002
Creative Education is an imprint of The Creative Company
www.thecreativecompany.us

Book and cover design by Blue Design (www.bluedes.com)
Art direction by Rita Marshall
Printed by Corporate Graphics in the United States of America

Photographs by Corbis (Louie Psihoyos/Science Faction), Dreamstime (Rosco), Getty Images (Brian Bahr, David Drapkin, Focus On Sport, Nick Laham, Jim McIsaac, Vic Milton/NFL, Darryl Norenberg/NFL, Rick Stewart, Rob Tringali/Sportschrome, Lou Witt/NFL)

Library of Congress Cataloging-in-Publication Data

Frisch, Aaron.
New York Jets / by Aaron Frisch.
p. cm. — (Super Bowl champions)
Includes index.
Summary: An elementary look at the New York Jets professional football team, including its formation in 1960, most memorable players, Super Bowl championship, and stars of today.
ISBN 978-1-60818-024-0
1. New York Jets (Football team)—Juvenile literature. I. Title. II. Series.

GV956.N42F75 2011
796.332'64097471—dc22   2010001021

CPSIA: 040110 PO1141

First Edition
9 8 7 6 5 4 3 2 1

CONTENTS

SUPER BOWL CHAMPIONS

New York is a city in the state of New York. It has a lot of sports teams and is nicknamed "The Big Apple." The New York City area has a **stadium** called New Meadowlands Stadium that is the home of a football team called the Jets.

JETS FACTS

First season:
1960

Conference/division:
American Football Conference, East Division

Super Bowl championship:
III, January 12, 1969
16–7 versus Baltimore Colts

Training camp location:
Cortland, New York

NFL Web site for kids:
http://nflrush.com

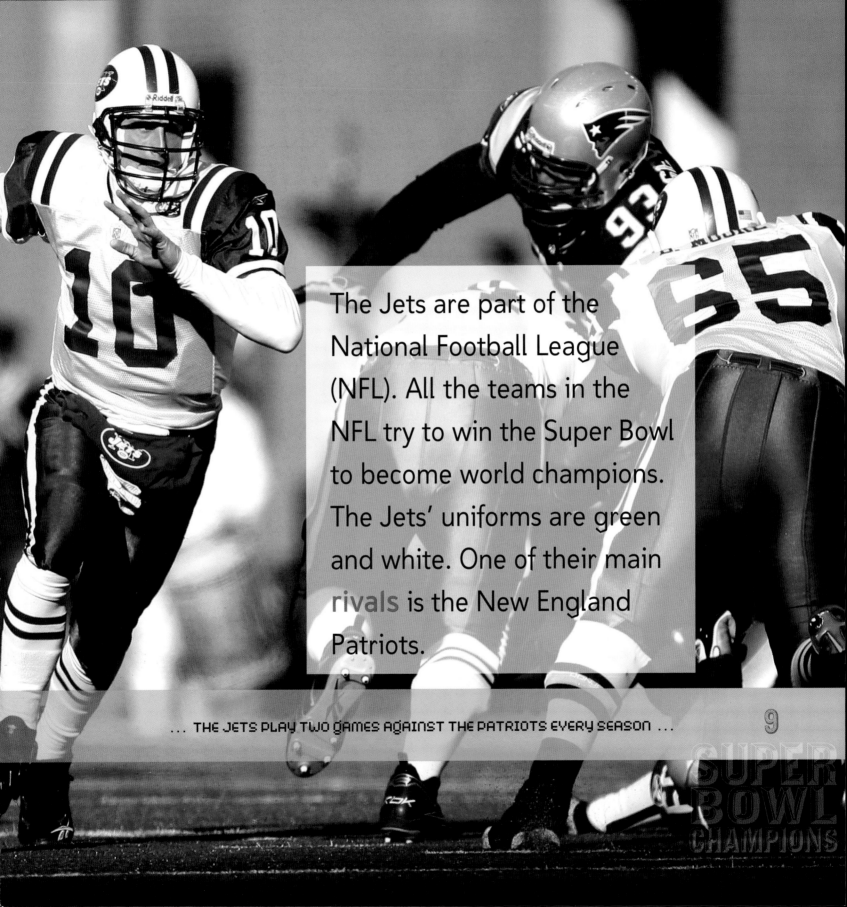

The Jets are part of the National Football League (NFL). All the teams in the NFL try to win the Super Bowl to become world champions. The Jets' uniforms are green and white. One of their main rivals is the New England Patriots.

... THE JETS PLAY TWO GAMES AGAINST THE PATRIOTS EVERY SEASON ...

9

The Jets played their first season in 1960. They were called the Titans at first. They were part of a different **league** called the American Football League then. The Titans lost a lot games.

10

SUPER BOWL CHAMPIONS

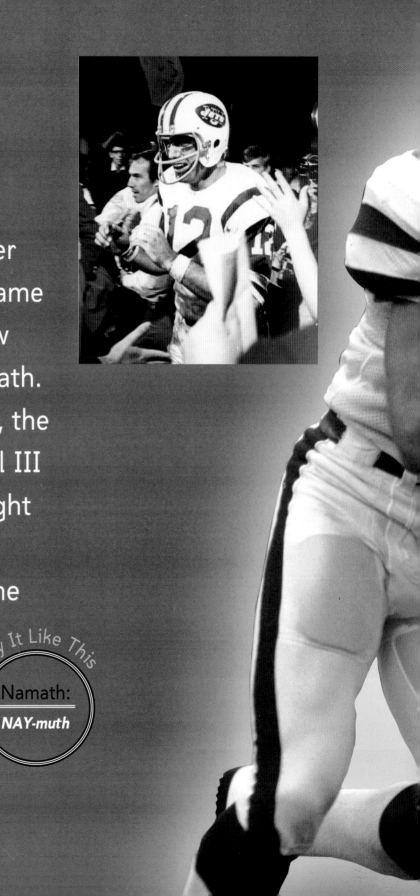

The team got better when it changed its name to Jets and added new quarterback Joe Namath. After the 1968 season, the Jets got to Super Bowl III (3). Most people thought they would lose to the Baltimore Colts. But the Jets won, 16–7!

Say It Like This

Namath:

NAY-muth

12

SUPER BOWL CHAMPIONS

Gastineau:

GAS-tih-noh

The Jets were not very good in the 1970s. But in the 1980s, they added new players like fast defensive end Mark Gastineau. He helped New York get to the **playoffs** four times.

... JOE NAMATH (LEFT) AND MARK GASTINEAU (RIGHT) ...

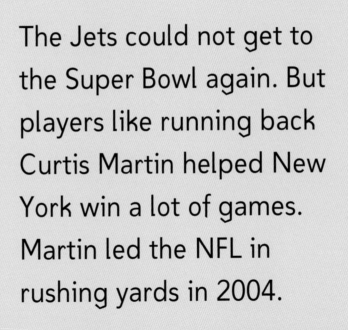

The Jets could not get to the Super Bowl again. But players like running back Curtis Martin helped New York win a lot of games. Martin led the NFL in rushing yards in 2004.

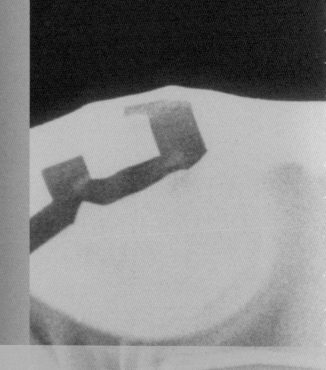

The Jets have had many stars. Matt Snell was a tough running back who helped the Jets win Super Bowl III. Defensive tackle Joe Klecko helped Mark Gastineau make many quarterback sacks.

... JOE KLECKO PLAYED MANY GREAT GAMES IN THE 1970S AND 1980S ...

17

WHY ARE THEY CALLED THE JETS?

New York's team was called the Titans at first. (A Titan is a huge creature like a giant.) In 1963, the name was changed to Jets. The team's stadium was close to an airport, and jets often flew overhead during games.

SUPER BOWL CHAMPIONS

Say It Like This

Chrebet:
kreh-BET

Scrappy wide receiver Wayne Chrebet joined the Jets in 1995. He played in New York for 11 seasons. Center Kevin Mawae was another Jets star. He played in the **Pro Bowl** every year from 1999 to 2004.

Say It Like This

Mawae:
muh-WY

... WAYNE CHREBET WAS A TOUGH PLAYER AND A FAN FAVORITE ...

19

... MARK SANCHEZ HELPED THE JETS MAKE THE PLAYOFFS AFTER THE 2009 SEASON ...

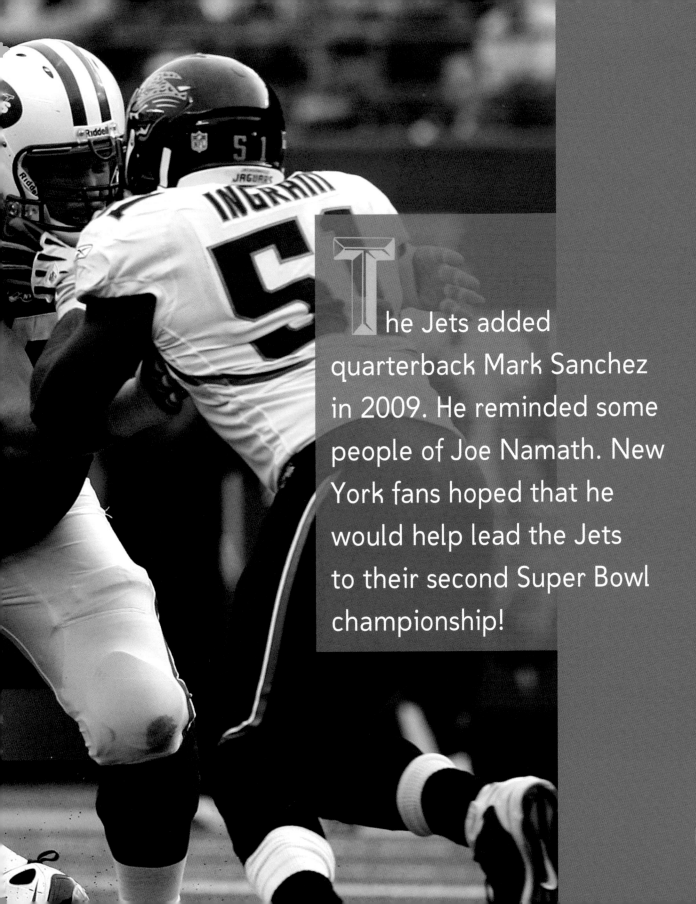

The Jets added quarterback Mark Sanchez in 2009. He reminded some people of Joe Namath. New York fans hoped that he would help lead the Jets to their second Super Bowl championship!

SUPER BOWL CHAMPIONS

SUPER BOWL CHAMPIONS

GLOSSARY

league — a group of teams that all play against each other

playoffs — games that the best teams play after a season to see who the champion will be

Pro Bowl — a special game after the season where only the NFL's best players get to play

rivals — teams that play extra hard against each other

sacks — plays where a player tackles a quarterback who is trying to throw a pass

stadium — a large building that has a sports field and many seats for fans

SUPER BOWL CHAMPIONS

INDEX

24